Drawing Fun

HOW TO DRAW Cool KIDS

by Kathryn Clay

illustrated by Anne Timmons

Capstone press

Mankato, Minnesota

Snap Books are published by Capstone Press,
1710 Roe Crest Drive, North Mankato, Minnesota 56003.
www.capstonepub.com

Printed in China.
102015   009292R

Library of Congress Cataloging-in-Publication Data
Clay, Kathryn.
    How to draw cool kids / by Kathryn Clay; illustrated by Anne Timmons.
    p. cm. — (Snap books. Drawing fun)
    Includes bibliographical references and index.
    Summary: "Lively text and fun illustrations describe how to draw cool kids" — Provided by publisher.
    ISBN-13: 978-1-4296-2304-9 (hardcover) - ISBN 978-1-4914-7917-9 (paperback)
    ISBN-10: 1-4296-2304-7 (hardcover)
    1. Children in art — Juvenile literature. 2. Drawing — Technique — Juvenile literature. I. Timmons, Anne.
II. Title. III. Series.
NC765.C573 2009
743.4'5 — dc22   2008032571

Credits
Juliette Peters, designer
Abbey Fitzgerald, colorist

Photo Credits
Capstone Press/TJ Thoraldson Digital Photography, 4 (pencil), 5 (all), 32 (pencil)

The author dedicates this book to Ellen, Micah, and Austin — three very cool kids.

Table of Contents

Getting Started

You're an artist in the making who sees the world as one big canvas. Your notebook is covered in sketches. You doodle on every scrap of paper you can find. With your talent and the step-by-step instructions in this book, you can start turning those doodles into masterpieces.

Maybe you want to draw fashion designs? Practice drawing the movie star in a dazzling gown. Would you rather work on exciting action shots? Try sketching the soccer star expertly moving a ball down the field. Do you prefer challenging group shots? Then check out all the different roles in the rock band.

Of course, there are many ways to show off your style. Once you've mastered some of the characters in this book, you'll be able to draw your own fun figures. Let your creative side loose, and see what kind of cool kids you can create.

Must-Have Materials

1. First you'll need something to draw on.
   Any blank, white paper will work well.

2. Pencils are a must for these drawing projects.
   Be sure to keep a bunch nearby.

3. Because sharp pencils make clean lines,
   you'll be sharpening those pencils a lot.
   Have a pencil sharpener handy.

4. Even the best artist needs to erase a line now
   and then. Pencil erasers wear out fast. A rubber
   or kneaded eraser will last much longer.

5. To make your drawings pop off the page,
   use colored pencils or markers.

Ballerina

Don't be fooled by the tights and the tutu. Ballerinas are experienced athletes. It takes strength and stamina to perform elegant arabesques and flawless pirouettes. This prima ballerina poses in a simple but graceful position.

Every great ballerina needs a place to perform. Draw a grand stage where she can show off her skills.

STEP 1

STEP 2

STEP 3

STEP 4

Cheerleader

Get ready to pump up the crowd. Cheerleaders are all about energy, excitement, and entertainment. Make sure this sideline supporter has a big, bright smile and two pom-poms to wave. She'll need them to celebrate her team's victory.

After you've drawn one cheerleader, you'll be able to draw a whole squad cheering on the team.

STEP 1

STEP 2

STEP 3

STEP 4

Hip–Hop Dancer

Breakers love to show off their fancy footwork.
This b-girl is no different. She knows how to impress
a crowd with a rollback freeze and a solid 6-step.

After drawing this dancer,
you can draw a whole crew
of breakers showing off
their moves.

STEP 1

STEP 2

STEP 3

STEP 4

Movie Star

Movie stars are known for their fabulous fashion sense. This leading lady is no different. She shows off her style in a sparkling designer dress. With an elegant updo and a little bit of bling, she's ready for any red-carpet event.

This diva never wears the same dress twice. Give her a new look by drawing her in a stylish, short dress.

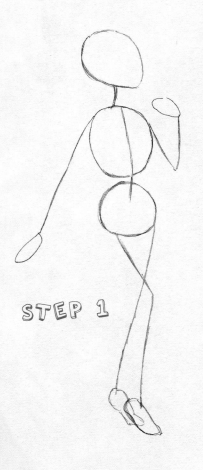

STEP 1

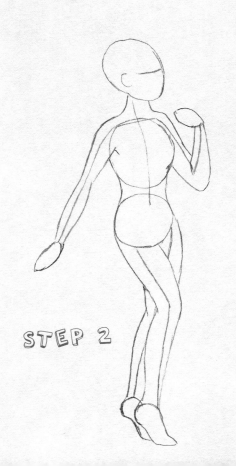

STEP 2

STEP 3

STEP 4

Trendsetter

This edgy girl loves to switch up her style. Sometimes that means adding red streaks in her hair and strapping on a pair of wings. While you never know what she'll be wearing, you can be sure it will be original.

Changing this cool kid's look is easy. Try drawing her in the wildest outfit you can imagine.

STEP 1

STEP 2

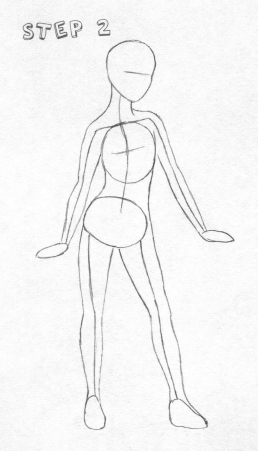

STEP 3

STEP 4

Prom Queen

For this dancing diva, it's all about the dress. A full-length formal is the best choice for prom. That way the dress twirls around her as she dances the night away. Add a sparkling tiara to top off her look.

This dancing queen doesn't want to dance alone. Draw a prom king to share the spotlight.

STEP 1

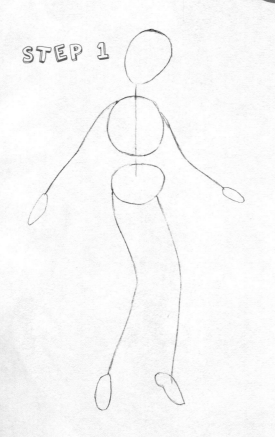

STEP 2

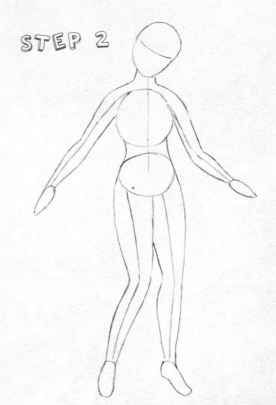

STEP 3

STEP 4

Skateboarder

You'll find this adventure-seeker testing her skills at the skatepark. She loves showing off kickflips and frontside boardslides. Here she's practicing a high-flying ollie — a popular skateboarding move.

This skater needs a place to work on her moves. Draw a skatepark with several steep ramps.

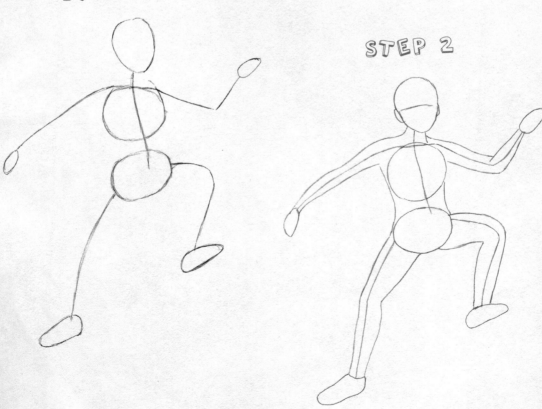

STEP 1

STEP 2

STEP 3

STEP 4

Soccer Star

This girl is dreaming about becoming the next Mia Hamm. Right now she's just practicing, but soon she'll be sailing shots into the net.

Draw a net and a goaltender so this player has a place to kick the ball.

STEP 1

STEP 2

STEP 3

STEP 4

Surfer

If the weather's warm and the waves are high, you'll find this guy at the beach. He's always on the lookout for the next big wave. But if he's not careful, he'll end up wiping out instead of hanging 10.

After you've mastered this drawing, try drawing a windsurfer. Just add a sail to the board.

STEP 1

STEP 2

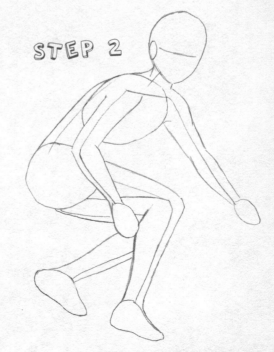

STEP 3

STEP 4

Yoga Girl

Being a kid can be stressful. This girl keeps her cool with long, deep breaths and a relaxing yoga pose. Draw her in loose, comfortable clothes that allow her to bend and twist easily.

Try drawing her in a more challenging pose like downward dog or half moon.

STEP 1

STEP 2

STEP 3

STEP 4

Rock Band

This group is ready to rock. The drummer provides a steady rhythm, while the guitar player adds an awesome melody. The lead singer rocks the mic. Now all they need is a gig.

Try drawing a few more band members. Add a bass player and a couple of backup singers.

STEP 1

STEP 2

STEP 3

To finish this drawing, turn to the next page. ⇨

STEP 4

STEP 5

Glossary

arabesque (air-uh-BESK) — a ballet move where the dancer stands on one leg and extends the other behind

b-girl (BEE-gurl) — a female breakdancer

gig (GIG) — a live performance in front of an audience

kickflip (KIK-flip) — a trick in which a skateboarder flips the board over during an ollie

ollie (AH-lee) — a trick in which a skateboarder steps on the back of the board to make the board rise into the air

pirouette (peer-OOH-et) — a ballet move where the dancer spins on one leg with the other leg in one of many positions